KEN ROBBINS

Air

THE ELEMENTS

HENRY HOLT AND COMPANY · NEW YORK

Henry Holt and Company, Inc.
Publishers since 1866
115 West 18th Street
New York, New York 10011

Henry Holt is a registered
trademark of Henry Holt and Company, Inc.

Published in Canada by Fitzhenry & Whiteside Ltd.,
195 Allstate Parkway, Markham, Ontario L3R 4T8.

Library of Congress Cataloging-in-Publication Data
Robbins, Ken. Air / Ken Robbins.
(The elements: 3)
1. Air—Juvenile literature.   [1. Air.]   I. Title.   II. Series:
Robbins, Ken. Elements: 3.   QC161.2.R63   1995   551.5—dc20   95-6692
ISBN 0-8050-2292-9

First Edition—1995

Printed in the United States of America
on acid-free paper. ∞

1   3   5   7   9   10   8   6   4   2

The photographs for this book are hand colored with water-based dyes.

For Meg Charlton

Anything that's thin and bright, clear, transparent, buoyant, light, insubstantial, subtle, soft or easy, the wind, a storm, the sighing breeze, breath itself, the sky, the thing without which fires die, the medium through which we smell and see, the cause of rust, the catalyst of energy—all these things the air can be.

BIG SKY, NEAR BOZEMAN, MONTANA

S K Y

DRAMATIC SKY, EAST HAMPTON, NEW YORK

Air is mostly nitrogen and oxygen and some carbon dioxide, too. There are also smatterings of pollen, pollution, bits of dust, and other kinds of matter. Air is a gas, it is our atmosphere, our sky, it has no shape, it has no size. It moves and flows, sinks when it's cold, and when it's hot, it rises. It has no taste and no color either, though you can hear it when the wind blows and you can feel it. You can see the stars through thirty thousand feet of air when the night is clear. But air also consists of clouds and fogs and mists and other things you can't see through. Taken all together, the conditions of the air are called the weather.

SKY

LONE OAK TREE, NEAR DAMARISCOTTA, MAINE

OXYGEN

The earth had an atmosphere billions of years ago, but it wasn't much like the one we know. There was methane and nitrogen and hydrogen in the air, but the crucial thing was that the oxygen wasn't there. It wasn't until the development of algae, plants, and trees that the air became something animals could breathe. Plants produce energy to live and grow. As they do, they manufacture oxygen and use up carbon dioxide, which is also called CO_2. None of us would be alive today if that weren't true, because with animals, it works the opposite way: we also produce energy, but when we do, we manufacture CO_2 and use up oxygen when we breathe. It's not a good idea to kill too many trees.

OXYGEN

FIVE BALLOONS, NASHVILLE, TENNESSEE

HOT AIR BALLOON

HOT AIR BALLOONS, NASHVILLE, TENNESSEE

Hot air rises and cold air sinks, because cold air is heavy and hot air is light. That
is the reason for the graceful flight of hot air balloons, which despite the immensity
of their bulk and size, float like angels in the sky.

   The entire system of weather we've got depends in like manner on what's cold and
what's hot. When the air gets heated by the sun or the earth, it rises and in so
doing gives birth to the endless cycles of wind and weather. The process is
known as the convection of air, which spreads the heat from here to the cold over
there.

CONVECTION

STORM OVER LAKE ABIQUIU, NEW MEXICO

<u>M O I S T U R E</u>

Water travels in rivers and streams, ocean currents, and in the tides. It also rides on currents of air, in the form of clouds. The winds push the clouds wherever they're blowing, and wherever the clouds go the water goes too. The clouds hold on to the moisture that's in them until a change in the temperature makes them let go. Then the sky opens up and the water falls down in one form or another: it could be rain—or else sleet, hail, or snow.

MOISTURE

TORNADO, WALNUT GROVE, MINNESOTA

HURRICANES AND TORNADOES

HURRICANE SEEN FROM SPACE

Hurricanes are spinning, circular, tropical storms; the eye in the center is always calm, but the winds at the edge are very strong, a hundred miles per hour or more. Hurricanes can knock down trees and telephone poles, smash windows, and bash in doors, a force of nature beyond control. Hurricanes are very wide, perhaps fifty miles from side to side. They move fairly slowly from place to place, and hurricanes can go on for days.

Tornadoes are even more violent storms; compared with hurricanes they're fairly small, and they rarely last very long at all. The violent, twisting, whirling winds of a tornado form a funnel-shaped cloud, the noise they make is appallingly loud, and when they touch down they can tear up everything on the ground, lifting up McGregor's car and dumping it in Johnson's yard.

HURRICANES AND TORNADOES

HOODOOS, NEAR DRUMHELLER, ALBERTA

<u>H O O D O O S   A N D   D U N E S</u>

CORAL PINK DUNES STATE PARK UTAH

Like all aspects of the weather, wind and water work together. Wind, like water, is a restless force, constantly moving and changing course. The wind picks up a handful of sand and flings it at a pile of rock, and tiny bits of the rock break off. Those tiny bits of rock are now more sand. They, too, now get blown around, and the wind may pile them into dunes and mounds. That's one of the ways that the earth breaks down and builds itself back up again. Of course, in the process the rocks are changed, they're scoured and sculpted and rearranged into shapes that are sometimes very strange.

HOODOOS AND DUNES

BELLOWS AND FORGE, FORT STEELE, BRITISH COLUMBIA

OXIDATION

RUSTED BOAT HULL, NEWPORT, OREGON

Everything in the world changes in time. Oxygen combines in several ways with substances of many kinds and changes them forever. Sometimes the change is slow, as when a large machine is left out in the weather. The iron it's made of joins with oxygen, which turns it into rust, and in a hundred years or so it's just a pile of dust.

Sometimes, though, the change is very fast—say, the way oxygen combines with coal to make a fire, and the fire turns the coal to ash. The more air that a fire gets the hotter it will be. A coal fire is very hot indeed (perhaps 500 degrees)—but still not hot enough for a blacksmith's needs. He can get the temperature much higher by using a bellows to blow air on the fire.

OXIDATION

RUGBY PLAYERS, EAST HAMPTON, NEW YORK

We inhale air for oxygen, and absorb it through our lungs, where it gets into our bloodstream and helps our bodies run. Machines burn fuel, and we burn food, that's how we get our energy; and when oxygen combines with food, the measure of the power produced is described in calories.

HUMAN ENERGY

YELLOW ROSE

Air is also important for what it carries. Airborne pollen makes some of us sneeze. Odors are carried along on the breeze. In fact, if we didn't have air we couldn't tell whether something even had a smell; because, when we breathe, it's air that carries the aroma of a rose and brings that sweet smell to our noses.

O D O R S

CLOTHESLINE, NANTUCKET, MASSACHUSSETTS

E V A P O R A T I O N

ELECTRIC FAN

When dry air passes over anything wet, the wetness changes into a gas, known as water vapor. Without this process (which is called evaporation) nothing wet would ever get dry; there would be no moisture in the sky; there would be no clouds, no fog, no rain; and if something got wet, it would stay that way.

Evaporation also has another effect: it cools. If you stand in front of a fan with your face all wet from getting in a sweat, the air from the fan will cool your face as it makes you dry, and evaporation is the reason why.

E V A P O R A T I O N

JET PLANES, AT SHIPROCK, NEW MEXICO

A I R P L A N E S

BIPLANE DUSTING CROPS NEAR FARGO, NORTH DAKOTA

As ocean liners sail the sea, airplanes sail the air. Air is a route for getting rapidly from here to there. Air is much thinner than water, so planes move more speedily through it. An old biplane, barely swifter than a car, might travel a hundred miles an hour, while a fast jet plane has so much power that it can go from New York to Chicago in the time it takes to watch a TV show.

AIRPLANES

FLOCK OF BLACKBIRDS, NEAR SHARON, CONNECTICUT

BIRDS

GOLDEN EAGLE YELLOWSTONE NATIONAL PARK, WYOMING

Though people can't fly without a plane, there are living things that can: insects buzz through empty air; germs and other tiny creatures float on the breeze; bats flit about by flapping their wings; and so do certain kinds of birds who flutter about among the trees and never try to fly too high. Other birds, like hawks and eagles, are masters of the sky. They can easily soar fifteen hundred feet or more above the land, riding the rolling, flowing currents of air.

BIRDS

SALSIFY PLANT, NEAR RONAN, MONTANA

S E E D   D I S P E R S I O N

DANDELION, LITITZ, PENNSYLVANIA

Certain plants, like dandelions, thistles, cotton, or milkweed, use the air to spread their seeds. Those seeds are usually connected to some fluffy stuff that will float along on a puff of breeze. That's how they're carried through the air, and when the wind dies down and the seeds alight, if the ground is fertile and the conditions right, a seed will take root (or at least it might) and another plant will grow.

SEED DISPERSION

METEOR, LEXINGTON, KENTUCKY

M E T E O R S

THE MOON FROM SPACE

The air is our shield, and our only protection against the constant bombardment of objects from space. The meteors or shooting stars that you can see in the night sky really are chunks of iron and rock from beyond our world that burn up in the air without leaving a trace. It's friction with the air that makes them burn, and if the atmosphere somehow weren't there, they would hit the earth with enormous force, creating giant holes in the ground, and fairly soon the surface of the earth would be covered with craters just like the moon.

METEORS

SUNBATHERS, NEWPORT, OREGON

RADIATION

The atmosphere absorbs some of the heat of the sun, making it possible for us to exist. Without it we'd surely be burnt to a crisp. Ozone is one of the gases in the air, and we have reason to be glad it's there because it filters the sun's ultraviolet rays. They are the ones that give you a tan, but they can also harm you in many ways. The ozone, however, is threatened these days by other pollutants we put into the air. They cause a chemical reaction that makes ozone disappear.

RADIATION

PREVAILING WINDS, WASHINGTON COAST

P R E V A I L I N G   W I N D S

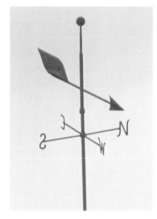

WEATHER VANE, NEW YORK

Sometimes the wind is just a momentary breeze, mussing our hair or rustling the leaves in fits and starts, but in certain parts of the world the wind is so steady, blowing from one direction day after day, that the trees all lean the opposite way.

The ancient Romans gave the winds names from the gods of their day, or perhaps it happened the other way; it's possible, too, that the gods got their names from the winds that blew. There's Boreas, the north wind; Zephyr, the west; Auster, the south wind; and Europe, the wind that blows from the east.

Sometimes from the mountains there is in winter a wind that's dry and hot. In the Alps of Europe it's called the foehn, but in different places it has a different name. In California it's called Santa Ana, and in Canada and parts of Montana it's called the chinook. The mistral in France is cold and raw, in South America they have the williwaw, and the sirocco is a hot desert wind in Morocco and other parts of Africa.

WINDMILL, NEAR STERLING, COLORADO

A steady wind is a useful thing. For centuries it's been a great source of mechanical power for pumping water or grinding grain into flour. The wind blows on the vanes of a windmill and spins them like a pinwheel, and those turning vanes can run machines. These days the wind can be used to make electric power—the very kind we need in this modern age.

W I N D M I L L

LATE START IN LIGHT AIR, SAG HARBOR, NEW YORK

A sailboat doesn't pollute and it doesn't make noise. It doesn't burn fuel, or require a motor; it glides for as long as the wind doesn't fail. For thousands of years, from our earliest days, sailors have prayed for the wind in their sails.

SAILBOATS

KITES AT THE BEACH, YACHATS, OREGON

K I T E S

With two sticks and some paper, and maybe a strip of rag for a tail, with a breeze, a place without too many trees, and a whole lot of twine, you can go fly a kite and see what it feels like to hold on to the wind at the end of a line.

KITES

SKYDIVERS IN FREE FALL, DRUMHELLER, ALBERTA

P A R A C H U T E S

PARACHUTIST LANDING, DRUMHELLER, ALBERTA

Air is not as thin as we might think. A falling man falls thirty feet in the time it takes that man to blink, but a parachute can grab the air and slow the man down so that he's falling gently by the time he hits the ground.

PARACHUTES

SKYLINE AND SMOG, SEATTLE, WASHINGTON

P O L L U T I O N

SUNSET AND SMOKE, MANHATTAN, NEW YORK

Fresh air is a precious natural resource; no one wants to ruin it, of course. In our haste to get rid of waste, though, in our hurry and our greed, we forget that there are consequences to everything we do, and too often we don't think them through. The smoke from our smokestacks, the exhaust from our cars, the soot from our chimneys, the toxic dust from nuclear tests, the fumes from the paint that we put on our walls—these become a part of our atmosphere and sooner or later we breathe them all.

POLLUTION

RAINBOW OVER PROMISED LAND, AMAGANSETT, NEW YORK

R A I N B O W

PRISM

The rainbow is a symbol of light, hope, and beauty, an archway of colors that glow in the sky. It occurs when the sun lights up the raindrops that are still in the air as a storm starts to clear. Light enters the raindrops, and when it's reflected it splits into colors of wonderful hue: red on the top side, then orange and yellow and green in the middle, then next comes the blue, and finally violet on the bottom or inside— and it all disappears in a minute or two.

RAINBOW

THE SUNWAPTA RIVER, JASPER NATIONAL PARK, ALBERTA

B R E A T H

MOUNTAIN GLORY, LAKE PLACID, NEW YORK

Without air, life would be impossible, and you and I would simply cease to be. But perhaps because air is a part of nature that we can't see, we take it for granted that air will always be there when we need it. Of course that isn't necessarily true, fresh air could turn out to be exceedingly rare. Much depends on what we humans do.

Some people say that with a puff of breath, God gave Adam life and death. Not everyone would put it just that way, but nearly everyone agrees that air is much more than something we need to survive, it's also a symbol of something divine. *Spiritus* was the ancient Latin word for breath. In our language it has come to mean spirit instead.

BREATH

Thanks to Dava Sobel for her manifest intelligence and enthusiasm; Gary Rieveschl for various crucial loanings from his collection of wonderful stuff; the estimable Michael and Louise, for inestimable friendship on the road; Faith Hamlin for her generous advocacy; Brenda Bowen for her excellent redaction; Martha Rago for her patience with megalomaniacal authors; and Maria for general life support. Christy Ottaviano and Theresa Park, whom I know mostly as intrepidly cheerful voices at the end of a phone line, never fail to be helpful as well.

Tornado photograph, on page 14, June 13, 1968, by Eric Lantz,
Walnut Grove Tribune, Walnut Grove, Minnesota.
Hurricane photograph on page 15 courtesy of NASA.
The blacksmith photograph on page 18 is of Paul Reimer, the
blacksmith at the Fort Steele Heritage Town, British Columbia
and was taken with his kind permission and cooperation.
Lunar photograph on page 31 courtesy of NASA.